THE NEWS MEDIA

THE NEWS MEDIA

BY RUTH AND MIKE WOLVERTON

FRANKLIN WATTS
New York/London/Toronto/Sydney/1981
A FIRST BOOK

Photographs courtesy of:
KVUE-TV, Austin Texas: pp. 13, 18, 37, 44;
Express News Corp., San Antonio, Texas: pp. 28, 31, 48;
KTVV-TV, Austin, Texas: pp. 15, 20;
United Press International: p. 25;
NASA: p. 54.

Library of Congress Cataloging in Publication Data

Wolverton, Ruth.
   The news media.

   (A First book)
   Bibliography: p.
   Includes index.
   SUMMARY: An introduction to the news media with emphasis on the tools and techniques used in developing a story.
   1. Journalism—Juvenile literature. [1. Journalism]
   I. Wolverton, Mike, joint author. II. Title.
PN4731.W64   070   80-25697
      ISBN 0-531-04194-8

Copyright © 1981 by Ruth and Mike Wolverton
All rights reserved
Printed in the United States of America
6 5 4 3 2 1

*To Jennifer Susan Hayes,
who has been a member
of the working press
since first grade*

And to Karelyn — a very special daughter and also a member of the media fraternity & sororities With our love
Mike Wolnick

To Karelyn with love
Ruth

CONTENTS

The News We See, Hear, and Read
1

How News is Discovered and Brought to Us
11

The News Media Twins
23

Developing a News Story
33

Tools and Techniques
43

How the News Affects Us
51

For Further Reading
57

Index
59

THE NEWS MEDIA

THE NEWS WE SEE, HEAR, AND READ

It began to rain suddenly at one o'clock Friday afternoon. It was one of those torrential rains that happen quite frequently in the summertime. It was nothing new.

By the time the city editor of the local newspaper got to his desk at three o'clock and settled into the routine of getting together the news for the next morning's early edition, the weather bureau was reporting that more than 3 inches (7.62 cm) of rain had fallen. But unless there was a lot more rain, most folks would have forgotten about the downpour by the time the early edition of the newspaper hit the streets at five o'clock, Saturday morning. The city editor stifled a yawn.

Across the city, the assignment editor at the television station checked the stories scheduled for the six o'clock news. They included reports of flash flooding at the usual low water crossings. So far, there was nothing very exciting about that.

An *anchorperson* (newscaster) at a city radio station finished her five minutes of hourly news at 3:05 P.M. with a weather report predicting that the rain was likely to continue and that the water level in the reservoir behind the city dam was rising rapidly. Something about that weather report made her feel uneasy. She went to the *morgue,* a filing cabinet in which all the old newscasts for the past two years were filed, and began to look for a story the station had reported on the dam many months ago. It was more of a hunch than anything else, but she was remembering that the U.S. Army Corps of Engineers had worked on the dam and somehow found it unsatisfactory . . .

"Probably grasping at straws," she told herself, "but on a dull news day, any straw in the wind is welcome."

WHAT IS NEWS?
Well, news doesn't always mean something completely new and different. News does not have to be something that has never happened before. We wouldn't have much news if that was the case. With the exception of such rare occasions as the first moon landing, or a brand new invention or discovery, the old saying that there is nothing new under the sun generally holds pretty true.

What we see on TV, read in the paper, and hear on the radio, and call "the news," are true stories about people's unusual experiences; warnings of danger to ourselves, our homes and businesses, our animals and plants, and important new information which helps us live our lives.

An unusual happening can be almost anything that is rare in a particular place at a given time. For instance, a lion walking down the street in New York City is definitely news. A lion walking along a road in Peru, Indiana would be unusual, too, but not as newsworthy since circuses often winter in Peru each year and lions do get out of their cages occasionally. In an African village, adjacent to a wildlife preserve with a large lion population, the story of a lion walking down the street would be news only if the lion happened to hurt or kill someone. By the same token, if you saw a donkey cart bumping along on the expressway in Detroit, Michigan, that would be news, but a donkey cart in a mountain village in South America is not news because everyone uses donkey carts to get about.

If there is a 2 inch (5.08 cm) snowfall in San Antonio, Texas, the news is proclaimed in big newspaper headlines and news bulletins on the radio and on TV. Why? Because in San Antonio it snows only once every ten years or so. A snowfall of 2 inches (5.08 cm) in Denver, Colorado, however, is not newsworthy because Denver has a lot of snow every winter. However, if there were a 2 inch (5.08 cm) snowfall in Denver on the Fourth of July, the mixture of snow and the Independence celebration would be news, since snow is rare in the summer, even in Colorado.

Some events and experiences are news everywhere, such as a long search for a lost child, a hijacking, a freak accident that injured or killed a large number of people, a natural disaster, such as an earthquake or flood, or a visit by a famous person. In fact, news doesn't have to be sad or frightening at all. It's news if someone wins a million dollars, is saved from a disaster, wins a medal at the Olympics, or collects more money than anyone else for a charity. It's news if someone has invented a new gadget, improved a machine, or figured out a different way to manufacture a product. It's news if scientists discover new facts about the human body, the age of Earth, or the composition of the planet Jupiter.

Another kind of news is information which helps people lead better lives. The latest reports on energy conservation help people decide which new heating system would be best for them. Stock market reports let people know which stocks are rising in value and would make a good investment. Consumer news informs people about goods and services and about defective models of vehicles or appliances that have had to be recalled.

News warnings not only inform the public about danger, potential or actual, but also advises them on what to do. They give alternate routes if there are road blockages, evacuation routes and procedures in case of disasters, and advice on how to secure homes and businesses to protect them as much as possible. The location of shelters and rescue crews is included when needed.

THE HISTORY OF NEWS

News, and the interest in news, isn't something that happened fairly recently with the advent of radio and television. It dates back a long time ago, before the first printing press was invented or a newspaper ever thought of—way before people had even invented writing.

People have always been interested in what happens to others. In olden times it was easy to keep up with the news in the village. All you had to do was go to the local well where the women were drawing water, or stop in at the men's meetinghouse and you could learn everything that had happened to everybody. It was a bit harder to find out what, if anything, of interest was going on in the village on the other side of the mountain. You had to wait until a hunting party encountered someone from over there, or make a special trip to find out. As a guest from a distant land, you became a source of news and gained instant status. Guests not only collected news, but they distributed it.

In addition to news about people, it was also important to hear whether the river was rising, whether the fish were running, if the forest fire was spreading, and who was on the warpath against whom.

For this reason, people developed a system of messengers and signals in order to carry information vital to survival across long distances. People traveled on foot and on horseback to carry news. Smoke signals were sent in some parts of the world, and drums were used to transmit news in others. Native Americans often drew pictures (called *pictographs*) on rocks to relay messages and news to other tribes traveling along the same routes.

Military expeditions and ship crews brought home news from distant places. More often than not, however, the news was "stale," because conditions had changed during the time it took to get the news from one place to another.

The circulation of written news had apparently begun independently at about the same time in ancient Rome and in Peking, China. Rome had a daily newspaper in circulation from its earliest days until its fall in A.D. 476. The *Acta Diurna* ("Daily Events") was in circulation to the general public, and was also used as a medium of communication between military officers and their armies. *Tsing-Pao* (the "Peking News") first appeared as a monthly publication in the sixth century. It contained imperial edicts and other official news, and did not cease publication until 1935. Early in the seventh century, the still-published *Peking Gazette* made its appearance.

After Johannes Gutenberg began printing from movable

type in Mainz, Germany, in about 1450, newspapers began to be circulated throughout Europe.

In 1690, Colonial America got its first newspaper, published in Boston, called, *Publick Occurrences, Both Foreign and Domestick*. Benjamin Franklin's *Pennsylvania Gazette* was published in Philadelphia weekly from 1729 until 1815.

During the nineteenth century, the invention of the telegraph and telephone changed news-gathering and reporting tremendously. The clicking of the telegraph key in New York City could relay a message almost instantaneously to a person in San Francisco, a whole continent away. With the advent of the transatlantic cable, news from Europe could be flashed to America, and vice versa, within a matter of minutes. The telephone allowed people to discuss happenings "person-to-person," though they might be thousands of miles apart.

The invention of the airplane early in this century enabled people to travel quickly to distant places. What happened in distant places then became important news to everyone.

Because of our rapid systems of transportation and communications, our entire planet has become a world where everything is somehow connected to everything else. Today we are quite literally connected to all parts of the world via satellites hanging 23,000 miles (36,720 km) out in space. These satellites orbit at a speed exactly equal to the speed at which the earth turns, and so remain suspended above the same place at all times. Television and radio news reports, and even entire pages of newspapers and news magazines, are sent around the world in only a fraction of a second, using several of these satellites in geostationary orbits.

HOW NEWS BECOMES HISTORY

When the news is "hot," that is, when a news story first breaks, we usually get it in the form of *news flashes,* brief statements that tell us what has just happened. As the story unfolds and more facts become known, reporters bring us the story during regular newscasts often directly from the scene. The anchorperson on radio or on television will announce that, "We take you now to . . . ," and the next thing you see will be a person in the next city, or the next country, or on the other side of the world, or even on the moon, telling you all about the story right from the place where it is happening.

Newspapers will carry the story in a *special edition* if it is vitally important, or on the front page of one of their regular editions. Newspapers will often have from two to six editions in a single day, mostly changing the front page in order to keep pace with fast-breaking news. Newspapers will go into much greater detail than radio or television newscasts do, with much "background" material so as to provide a better understanding of the story.

This, of course, is where history begins.

For the next day or two, or for as long as the story is "alive," further details and developments will be reported on the newscasts and written up in the daily papers. *Weekly news magazines* will also cover the story, in detail, and with background information that helps us put together the pieces and see a whole picture.

Finally, the event ends its life as "news," and enters its incarnation as "history."

There is one important difference between news and history, however. History is not just a collection of old news. While historians—the people who write history—do rely on news reports and the work of journalists, they do not give the same emphasis to events that the news reporters and editors do. It is often difficult to predict how important a news event will be several years from now. Events that may seem very important at the time they happen may turn out to be relatively unimportant when compared to the news of the next week or next month. More often, though, it is the other way around. Events that seem to be hardly newsworthy at all at the time, later on may turn out to be turning points in history. For example, on December 1, 1955, Mrs. Rosa Parks, a middle-aged black woman in Montgomery, Alabama, was ordered by a city bus driver to get up and give her seat to a white passenger. Refusing to do that, Mrs. Parks was arrested and fined ten dollars. That incident did not even get mentioned in any newspaper or on any radio station or TV station at the time it happened. But it is now written up in all the history books as the incident that triggered the famous bus boycott in Montgomery, Alabama, which ignited the great civil rights movement in the late 1950s—a worldwide news event that changed the course of American history. That is why nearly all events, especially if they are in some way related to the problems of the times, get at least some attention from the people who discover the news and bring it to us.

That is why even a Friday afternoon rainstorm got some attention.

The anchorperson at the city radio station found what she had been looking for in the morgue. It was an old news story about how the U.S. Army Corps of Engineers had made some temporary repairs on the city dam that impounded a huge reservoir, or lake, of water. But they had warned officials in the city that the dam might not be safe, in spite of the repairs, if very rapidly rising water built up quickly behind the dam. And that was exactly what was happening now!

The anchorperson quickly put in a phone call to the nearest office of the U.S. Army Corps of Engineers. She would try to get some more information about how much extra water the dam could hold. Then, she began to write a story for her four o'clock newscast that would inform her listeners about the fact that experts had said the city dam was not very safe.

The rain continued to come down in torrents.

HOW NEWS IS DISCOVERED AND BROUGHT TO US

Like the anchorperson at the city radio station, the people involved in collecting and spreading the news are called *journalists*. There are *print journalists* and *broadcast journalists*. Basically their task is the same. It is to find the news that is important to you and members of your community, and to bring the news to you as quickly and accurately as possible.

Good journalists are by nature curious and fascinated with everything that happens to other people. They are willing to spend long hours waiting for a story to break. They will wade through mud; suffer cold, hunger or thirst if need be, all to "get the story."

Covering, or discovering, the news, is a great adventure and a demanding job. Not only do journalists have to be persistent, but they also need to have a good fund of general knowledge about people, things, and events, and to be able to research a story completely. Journalists should be able to write a story concisely—that is, to include all the important facts and to cut out all unnecessary material.

In the course of their work, most journalists develop the

all-important habit of asking many questions. At first, they may feel bashful or even silly, asking people all these questions. But journalists soon learn that only by asking questions of all kinds, even questions to which they think they may already know the answers, will they get all the information they need in order to write or to broadcast their stories. Asking the right questions at the right time also helps journalists discover story leads and makes it possible for them to be on the scene when a news story is about to break.

THE PEOPLE WHO BRING YOU THE NEWS

How and where do journalists find the news?

In every city, small town, or village, and in many rural areas as well, there are people called *stringers* who work for local or big city newspapers, radio, or TV stations. In fact, many young people get a start in journalism by "stringing." The stringers keep a sharp eye out for what goes on in their small corner of the world. This includes all the daily happenings in local government, politics, schools, and the lives of the people in the community. If something out of the ordinary occurs—if, for instance, a local politician announces she is going to run for governor, or the owner of the local Ford agency is taken hostage in a hijacking, or a local boy scout troop is missing in a blizzard, the stringer will immediately "tip-off" his editor at the newspaper or broadcast station. He will do the same in case of warnings. If a tornado is sighted or there is a sudden rise in the local creek, it might indicate a flash flood upstream. The stringer will call his editor and tell him what is going on. If the editor decides that the story is important enough, he will tell the stringer

A television news reporter and his cameraman check the videotape of a news event. They can see a playback of the tape they have just made by looking in the viewfinder of the camera.

to gather up all the information he can find and phone it in as soon as possible. If it looks like a really big story, the editor will send out a reporter to help cover the story.

Reporters are usually assigned to a *beat,* a special area of news coverage. One reporter might be on the police beat, or the *cop shop,* as they often call it, and that reporter will spend most of her time at the police station, or the sheriff's office. There, she'll hear about events involving the police the moment they happen. Other reporters cover City Hall, the county courthouse, the state legislature, Congress, or the residence of the president, or the prime minister of a country as their beat. Some reporters might draw a sports beat or a science news beat. Other reporters work on *general assignment,* which means that they are available to work on any story that needs coverage.

Reporters work in many different ways to get their stories. They may use the telephone, go out on the street and talk to people in person, interview specialists in many fields, and use books and magazines for additional information. And, like the anchorperson at the city radio station, they will consult the morgue file for facts and figures.

Reporters have to ask a lot of questions, but they have to know what questions to ask to get the particular information they need. When the reporter has collected all the facts for a story, she'll write it and send it into the editor. If time is short, she'll phone in the facts to a *rewrite person* who will then do the actual writing.

If the reporter is working for a radio or TV station, he may, after phoning in the story, ask for a camera or sound crew to come to the scene and record the story on tape.

After the story is finished, either written or taped, the editor

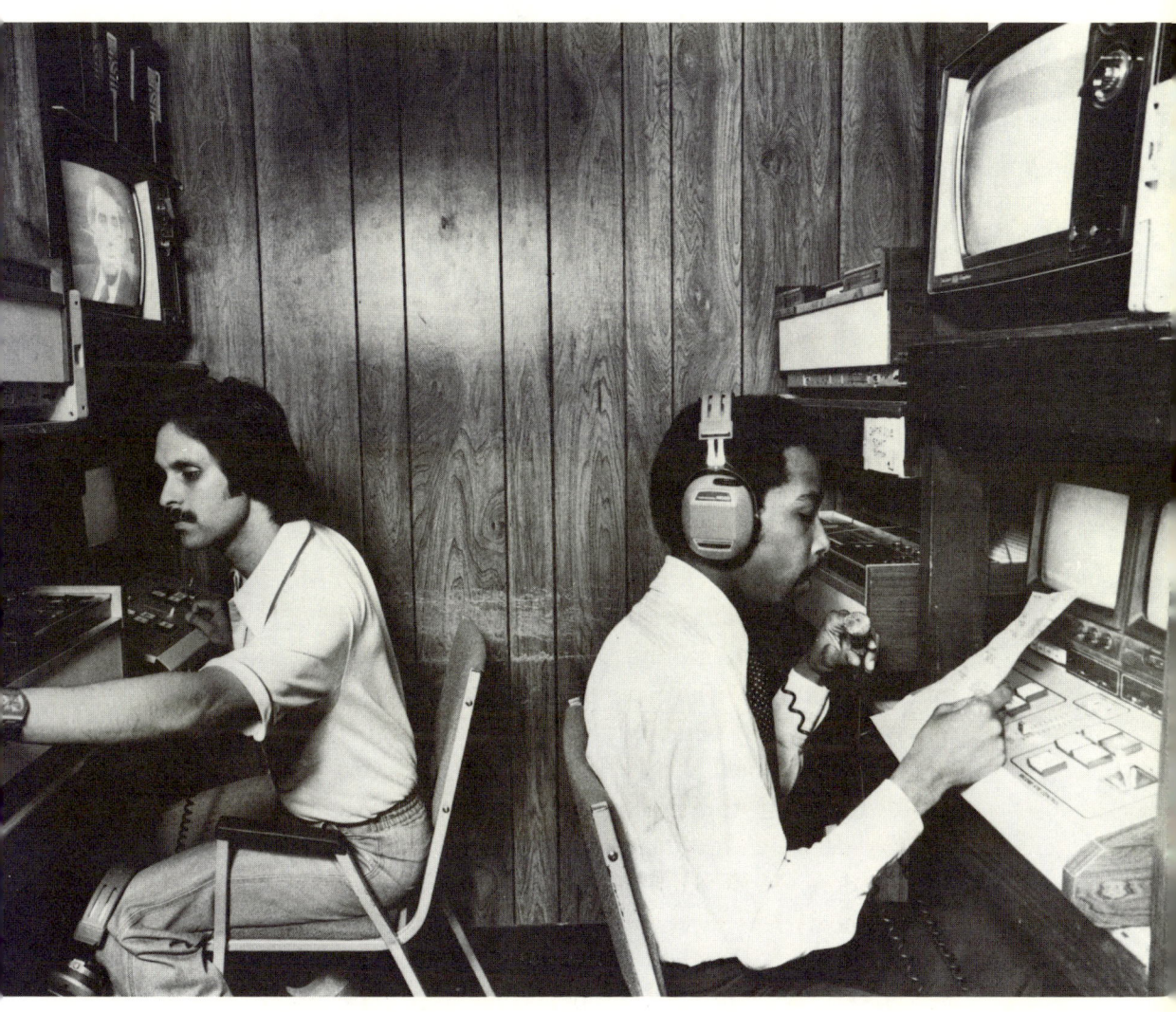

A television reporter (right) makes a "voice over" that will be used with a videotaped sequence of a news story.

at the newspaper or broadcast station will make the final decision about the space or time to be allowed for the story. The editor will also decide where the story will appear and whether or not related stories, called *side bars,* that help people to understand the main story better, will be used. The editor could even decide not to run the story at all.

Television networks and many newspapers send *special correspondents,* or reporters, to important news centers all over the world. There are correspondents in most of the larger capitals in Europe and Asia, as well as in any other place where interesting and important things happen often. Special correspondents send back stories from battlefronts, attend peace talks between hostile countries, and are at hand when spaceships are about to take off. A special correspondent often moves around a lot, spending one week in London, the weekend in Moscow, and the next week in Tokyo. Special correspondents have to have a great deal of background knowledge so that they can learn quickly all about what is going on at the moment and cover and write the story while it is "hot," or still developing.

Editors at newspapers and broadcast stations review all the stories turned in to them by their reporters and correspondents and decide which are the most important ones for their viewers and readers. Most editors make these important decisions by asking themselves these questions: Is the story about something that may be dangerous to the public? Is there something they need to know for protection? Is it something people will have to make a decision about or vote on in the next election? Is it something they could write to their representative about? Is it something that will help them in their daily lives?

NETWORKS, BUREAUS, AND WIRE SERVICES

Keeping up with the stories brought in by the staff is only part of an editor's job. An editor must also keep up with news from all over the world which comes into newspaper and radio and TV newsrooms on *teletype machines.* The teletypes carry the information gathered by worldwide news services.

Most individual radio or TV stations, as well as the smaller newspapers, can't afford to have special correspondents all over the world. Yet, they need to keep their readers and viewers informed about world affairs, as well as about what is going on both statewide and on the national scene. The news services and networks were organized to fill this need.

Three of the largest news services are the Associated Press (AP), United Press International (UPI), and Reuters International. The wire services maintain their own special correspondents and news bureaus throughout the world. News bureaus are permanent news-gathering facilities located in important places and staffed with reporters and editors. Each broadcast station or newspaper pays a monthly fee to support these news services, and in turn, receives one or more teletype machines for their newsroom. These teletypes run continuously, twenty-four hours a day, seven days a week. They type out news flashes, bulletins, warnings, stories, and even complete feature articles and news broadcasts, using material from all over the world. In turn, each *affiliate,* the newspaper or broadcast station that buys the news service, will "feed" news from its locality to the wire service, to be used on the teletype machines.

So much news is generated by the wire services that they

Large broadcast networks often send their national and international news stories to their local affiliated stations. Here the producer of a TV news program goes over the schedule of network news stories with a technician standing at the studio videotape machine.

have separate teletype machines for different news categories. They have machines over which they send only sports news, others for weather news, separate ones for national and international news, and still others for news of interest to a single state or region. Some large cities, like Chicago, have a separate circuit and teletype machine that carries only news about the city. These circuits with their own teletype machines are called *wires* for short, and are usually referred to as the *sports wire,* the *weather wire,* the *city wire,* and so on.

At most newspapers, editorial judgment—that is, the decision about what to print, is made jointly by the editors on the staff. The editors—city, state, national, financial, and so on—are called together once a day by the managing editor for a "budget meeting," or "big meeting," as it is often called. At that meeting, decisions are made about what stories will go on the front page. The editors also make sure that the big stories are satisfactorily covered. Each editor has a certain amount of space—a number of columns—to fill, as he or she sees fit.

Each editor will express preferences about which stories are important and how much space they should get. Often the city editor and the national editor will have differences of opinion about whether a certain story should have front-page space. At times, the financial editor might think a story should not be "buried" on the regular financial page, but printed "up front," on, or near, the front page of the paper. The managing editor settles such disputes and usually has the last word. The managing editor can be overruled only by the publisher of the paper.

Broadcast stations and networks go through a similar joint decision process. The producer of the newscast is the one who makes the final decision on what news stories will be aired on the next newscast.

The producer of a television newscast works with the news reporter to get the timing of a news story just right.

The city editor of the local newspaper had not heard the four o'clock newscast on the radio. He missed the story about the trouble with the dam the anchorperson had resurrected from her morgue file. But the city editor had already sent one of his staff members to search the morgue at the newspaper office for any background information that might be needed if the heavy rains continued. Water pressure was even then building up behind the dam. The city editor, too, remembered that although the dam had had some recent repair work, it was not as strong as it ought to be. In fact, the editor had a feeling that if the rain continued to pour down at the rate the weather bureau was reporting, the city dam could be the big news story by morning.

That feeling was shared not only by the editor at the radio station, but by the assignment editor at the television station as well, who at 4:30 P.M. heard from his news van that some of the city streets were flooding. There was no sign that the pouring rain would stop soon.

THE NEWS MEDIA TWINS

The business of reporting the news is divided between the news media "twins," broadcasting and print.

BROADCAST NEWS—
TV AND RADIO

The broadcasting media includes radio and television.

On radio, there are usually five-minute news reports every hour during the day, and blocks of news that may last from thirty minutes to two hours, which are aired during the time most people are driving to and from work. This so-called "drive time" is usually considered to be between 7:00 A.M. and 9:00 A.M., and from 4:00 P.M. to 6:00 P.M. These drive time blocks will have international, national, state, and local news reports, one after the other. These reports will include segments on sports, weather, and the latest on traffic conditions. The news reports usually consist of straight voice reports by the anchorperson at the station, which he or she reads to you from written copy. Often these voice reports will be interspersed with *actualities,* which are tape-recorded reports or statements direct from the scene of the news action. Actualities can consist of the voices of the actual people involved in the news story, on-the-scene reports, and interviews with important people who might have inside information about a story.

Documentaries, reports that cover a news story from many different angles, are also used at times. In many cases, radio documentaries are broken up into five-minute segments and broadcast one segment per hour during the entire broadcast day.

In some cities, there are radio stations that broadcast nothing but news, one newscast back-to-back with the next. These stations have been quite successful, and much to the surprise of some, people will actually stay tuned to the all-news station to keep on top of what is happening out in the world, and to get the news in greater detail while they go about their work, all day and all night long.

Regularly scheduled television newscasts are usually thirty minutes to one hour long, but special reports may run as long as ninety minutes. In addition, one-minute reports called *newsbreaks* are broadcast hourly by some stations and networks. Some pay-TV subscribers on cable television are able to receive an all-news television channel.

On commercial and public television, newscasts are aired in the early morning, early evening, and late evening. Many individual television stations also have noontime news programs. TV newscasts are usually anchored by a prominent news personality—sometimes two or even three—especially at the network level. At the local level, there is usually a "team," consisting of one or more anchorpersons, a weather person, and a sportscaster. These teams and the network anchorpersons cover what they and their producers, editors, and reporters feel is the important news of the day. They make use of reports, interviews,

Susan Stamberg, co-host of "All Things Considered," interviewed President Jimmy Carter in October 1979 for a live broadcast on National Public Radio.

and on-the-scene action videotaped in all parts of the world and sent into the newsrooms via satellite and *microwave*.

The anchorpersons supply background information for these reports and tie them all together. Often the anchorperson will read a report for which there is no video, using instead artwork that appears on a screen behind him or her. This keying in of artwork and pictures serves the purpose of keeping the audience informed on what the story being broadcast is all about. A story about nuclear energy, for example, might have a drawing of an atom being split, keyed in behind the anchorperson.

Special news reports generally follow the same format and are used to report on stories so lengthy or complex that they cannot be covered satisfactorily on the regularly scheduled news broadcasts. Television news documentaries are similar to special reports except that they tend to deal with the documentation of a news story after it has played out as news, and has become part of our history.

The television news *magazine* treats current ongoing news stories in a documentary fashion, but presents three or four such mini-documentaries in each program. These programs (such as *Sixty Minutes*) are called magazines because, like magazines, they contain several feature stories per "issue."

PRINT NEWS—
NEWSPAPERS
Big newspaper offices are busy, twenty-four hours a day, seven days a week. Reporters, editors, and the many people who run the typesetting computers and presses work in shifts so that their readers will not miss the news of any of the important events that happen in the world.

In newspapers, space is allotted to a story according to its importance and special interest. An important story which affects and interests most readers will be a front-page story with big headlines *above the fold,* that is, on the top part of the front page where it can be seen when the newspaper is folded in half. Stories a little less important would go on the front page with headlines in smaller type *below the fold.* Follow-up stories and reports of less immediacy, but of great importance, dealing with international, national, or local issues, will make up the rest of the first section of the paper. Section two, in most dailies, carries the city and local news—again with the most important stories on the section's front page and the less important stories in the rest. Business news, both national and local, is often also included in that section. Section three is usually a feature section. It carries information about what people in your town are doing, interesting activities, personality profiles, and notices of forthcoming events and entertainment. Often this section will include reports by amusement editors on new plays being performed in town, new motion pictures which have opened, or concerts that have been held. TV and radio program guides are also often part of the local feature section. Section four may be the sports section which covers all the hard sports news, as well as features on players and games, and predictions about the probable outcome of future events based on interviews with coaches and managers. In most papers, section five contains classified "ads" including news about available jobs, cars, and other merchandise available to be bought, business opportunities, lost-and-found objects, and real estate offered for rent, lease, or sale.

In addition to the factual stories that make up the bulk of the newspapers and broadcast news reports, both media twins

usually offer some opinions based on the news. These are the *editorials*.

Many publishers employ editorial writers to write daily opinions for the public to read. This is called the editorial *slant* of the newspaper. While good publishers will not let their personal opinions affect their paper's coverage of the news, the editorial opinions of the publisher will be made obvious on the editorial page or pages of the paper. Most newspapers also publish opinions of their readers in a *letters to the editor* column.

Some editors or other writers who are particularly knowledgeable on a given subject, will write a series of opinion pieces. Because these pieces are usually printed in one long vertical segment of the newspaper, they are called *columns,* and their authors are called *columnists*. Not all columns deal with serious or vital issues. Erma Bombeck and Peggy Bracken, for instance, have become famous for their humorous columns. Heloise is known all over the country for her helpful advice and household hints. Columnists Ann Landers and Amy Vanderbilt have become our national guidelines for personal conduct.

Unlike newspapers, broadcast stations cannot be opinion platforms for their owners. That is because the airwaves belong to the public and so the government must regulate them. Anyone can start a newspaper—it does not require any license from

The pressmen in the pressroom of a daily newspaper check the papers as they come already folded off a high-speed printing press.

the government. Not everyone, however, can get a license to operate a broadcast station because space in the radio and television bands is very limited. Those who are fortunate enough to get a license must treat it as a public trust and open up their broadcast frequency to all types of public opinion. This government policy is called the Fairness Doctrine. It prohibits a broadcast station owner from expressing editorial opinions without offering *equal time* to the expression of opposing views and opinions.

There are other differences between the print and broadcast media twins that are significant. The print media carry much more news every day than does either radio or TV. In fact, if all the news broadcast in one day by any one radio or TV station were printed in a newspaper, it would amount only to a few pages at most. Perhaps that is why Walter Cronkite, the famous CBS news anchorperson, once said that when he signs off his news broadcast, he often wishes he could tell his viewers to go and read their newspapers to find out more details about the day's news.

TV and radio, however, have the advantage of bringing you the news in the form of bulletins and news flashes almost as soon as it happens anywhere in the world. TV can bring you the picture and sound of an event as it is happening.

There are many similarities between the media twins, too, of course. Both news media use highly complicated electronic

The composing room in a newspaper office is where newspaper pages are laid out to be photographed onto metal plates for printing.

gadgets to save money and time in the business of bringing you the news as quickly and accurately as possible. The print media use the very latest computers to compose the pages and set up those even columns and margins that you see in any newspaper or news magazine. The broadcast media work with a whole array of electronic apparatus including video and audio tape recorders, monitors and mixers, and relays, to get the news to your radio or TV set as rapidly as possible. The publishers and producers in both media are constantly on the lookout for new advancements in electronic equipment that can be used to do the job of news-gathering and distributing better and even faster. When a news story does break, it is often something the public needs to know about in a hurry. Hours and even minutes saved in getting the news out can often mean the difference between life and death.

DEVELOPING A NEWS STORY

News of the impending dam disaster first came out of the cop shop in the city. A police reporter for the newspaper got her lead while going over some routine police reports in the pressroom at the police station. The police sergeant in charge of public relations told the reporter that the U.S. Army Corps of Engineers had informed the mayor and the police chief that the dam was in danger of collapsing, and that residents and campers below the dam had to be evacuated before dawn.

Almost at the same time that the newspaper reporter called her editor on duty at the city desk to give him the dam story, a radio reporter phoned his newsroom from the county sheriff's office, which was his regular beat, and reported the same story. A few minutes later, at the TV station, a long-distance call from the state capital reporter alerted the news staff that the governor was preparing to put the state militia immediately on standby alert in view of the danger to the dam.

The radio station was the first to break the news to the public. It was ten minutes to five in the evening when the sheriff came into the pressroom at the county courthouse and told the radio newsreporter about the potential danger. The radio station had a five-minute newscast scheduled on the hour, every hour. This gave the reporter ten minutes until his next deadline—plenty of time to turn on his cassette recorder and ask the sheriff to read his statement into the microphone.

"*The U.S. Army Corps of Engineers is asking residents and vacationers living, working, and playing below the city dam, to seek higher ground immediately,*" the sheriff said. "*The unusually heavy rainfall in a short period of time has caused pressures on the dam that it may not be able to withstand. All persons downstream from the dam are asked to begin evacuation immediately.*"

The reporter quickly wrote a *lead-in* to the sheriff's statement, and then called his newsroom on the telephone.

"Got a hot one for you," he told the anchorwoman on the other end of the phone line. "Stand by." He played his cassette recorder into the telephone line and then gave a brief countdown.

"Three, two, one. *River City residents have just been warned by Sheriff Ed Burr that the thirty-year-old dam impounding the waters of City Lake may not last the night. Sheriff Burr told this reporter just moments ago. . . .*" The reporter pushed the play button on his cassette recorder and the sheriff's voice came on the line with the statement he had just recorded. When the sheriff finished speaking, the reporter signed off with a brisk, "*Chris Wolf reporting from the county courthouse for Action News.*"

The anchorwoman at the radio station recorded both the reporter's *voicer*—his lead-in statement, and his actuality, the sheriff's voice—onto a tape cartridge which she would insert into the five o'clock newscast. The story was ready to go on the air a full two minutes before the five o'clock deadline. Just before going on the air, the anchorwoman called the news director on the intercom and told him about the dam story.

The news director, who doubled as the assignment editor, immediately called his reporter at the sheriff's office. The reporter was hard at work putting together the new developments on the dam story—updating the story for the six o'clock newscast with reports from the sheriff's officers coming in from the threatened area. The news director and the reporter agreed that the latter should stay close to the sheriff, his source for official information, and at the same time, keep up with the latest from the dam site through the coming and going of the sheriff's officers.

Next, the radio news director got on his two-way radio, contacted a reporter on his way to the monthly meeting of the City Planning Commission. He told the reporter to skip the meeting, head out to the dam, and get some statements from the U.S. Army Corps of Engineers about the actual threat to the county recreation area and to the city itself.

Then, the news director told the anchorwoman about these assignments, suggested several phone calls for additional information that could be made from the newsroom, recommended that she pass the dam story onto the regional network and feed it to the wire service, and asked for thirty-second bulletins on it on the half hour.

Finally, the news director picked up his cassette recorder, got his car out of the lot, and headed out to the threatened area. He planned to interview the people who had been asked to leave their homes, to cover the actual evacuation, and to develop his station's coverage of the story using a two-way radio from the scene.

"EVACUATE!"

Meanwhile, the assignment editor at the television station had one hour and five minutes until the six o'clock news was scheduled to go on the air when his reporter called in from the state capital. She had a videotape of the governor and a stand-up report delivered in front of the office of the commander of the state militia.

"The governor has called out the militia," she told her editor, "and ordered them into the area below the city dam to help get everyone out of there. She's been told by the U.S. Army Corps of Engineers that the city dam is likely to break before daylight."

After a brief consultation with the producer of the six o'clock news, the assignment editor instructed his crew at the state capital to put their tape on the next flight into the city which was scheduled to arrive there within the hour. Then the crew was to work on an in-depth report on the progress of the evacuation of the recreation and residential area below the dam from the state militia's command post for the ten o'clock news.

This microwave van enables reporters to send the film and sound of a news event, as it is actually happening, back to the studio for broadcast.

Next, the TV station assignment editor sent another of the station's news crews out to the dam site and recreational area to report on how the evacuation was actually working—again for the ten o'clock news. He dispatched the station's microwave van with its videotape playback machine to the airport to await the arrival of the governor, taped a few minutes before six o'clock. Since there wouldn't be time to take the tape back to the station, it was to be played back from the van so it could be seen on the six o'clock news. After that interview, the van was to meet the crew at the dam site in order to send in their reports from there via microwave for the ten o'clock news.

Finally, the assignment editor ordered that a *crawl* be keyed in on the ongoing program, giving the viewers a news flash of the developing dam story. And so, without missing any of their regular programs, viewers could keep up with the latest developments by reading the statements that moved or "crawled" across the bottom of their TV picture tube, informing them about the progress of the evacuation.

The *city editor* of the newspaper was seven hours and ten minutes away from his midnight deadline for the morning edition, when his police beat reporter called in. After telling the reporter to send out for a hamburger and stay with the story at the cop shop, the city editor called two of his general assignment reporters to his desk. He dispatched one to the dam site recreation area to get the story on the condition of the dam and the progress of the evacuation, and told him to take a photographer along. The other reporter was instructed to find some high-ranking officer with the U.S. Army Corps of Engineers, and get a story on the probabilities of the dam holding, and what might happen if it did not. Then, the city editor called in the paper's science reporter-editor and asked her to research a recent U.S. Corps of Engineers report on the dam and find out what had been done, if anything, about repairing the dam.

The state news editor stopped by the city editor's desk with a story on the governor's action, just as a copy girl laid the first wire service copy on the story, fresh off the paper's teletype machines, on the city editor's desk. The editor read the story quickly.

"Governor Charlotte McLellen, acting on advice from the commanding general of the U.S. Army Corps of Engineers, has ordered the state's militia troops into River City to aid in the evacuation of some 50,000 persons from the low-lying areas below the old River City Dam.

"It is the opinion of engineers and scientists who have inspected the dam," said Governor McLellen, "that it cannot hold back the rapidly rising water if rainfall in excess of one inch [2.64 cm] per hour continues throughout the night.

"Both city and county residents, and especially visitors to the state recreational areas downstream from City Lake, are urged to seek safety on high ground above the dam.

"The National Guard Armory has been opened to provide shelter and food for those in need of it . . ."

The managing editor of the newspaper was about to leave for the day, when the city editor and state editor came into his office for permission to remake the front page of the morning edition. The entire paper had been made up at the budget meeting earlier in the day, but with the dam story developing as it was, they would have to put it on the front page and pull some of the stories already planned for it. Quickly, the three reworked the space budget for the morning edition and passed on the information on the new layout to the composing room and print shop.

Back at his desk, the city editor assigned a rewrite person to stay close to the telephone *hot line* to write news stories just as quickly as the reporters could phone in the facts. The reporters were to stay on their beats, so they needed someone at the paper to type up their stories for the deadline.

The dam story remained the top story all through the evening. At the radio station, *advisories* had been inserted into the regular programming every fifteen minutes, which gave the location of shelters for the evacuees and other pertinent information. News bulletins continued to be broadcast at the half hour, and in the regular newscast on the hour. Updated stories on the dam situation and the evacuation filled most of the air time.

When the ten o'clock news came on TV, the viewers received on-the-scene reports from the dam site. In addition, the anchorperson had a story from the U.S. Army Corps of Engineers, which indicated that the threatened dam was one of the seventeen dams that the U.S. Bureau of Reclamation had listed several years ago as being in need of modification in order to withstand heavy floods. The weatherperson added his contribution to the story, a hopeful note, this time. The torrential rains seemed to be slackening and a high-pressure front was moving into the area faster than had been expected.

The TV station continued to key in a crawl over the scheduled programming every fifteen minutes to advise on shelters and other necessary information for the evacuees. In addition, a bulletin was inserted on the half hour and the dam story was updated on the regular hourly newsbreaks.

At the newspaper, the science reporter finished her research a few minutes after ten. She had spent the time in between studying news reports about dams in general and the endangered one in particular in the newspaper morgue. She had gotten a number of good leads from the material, made a dozen follow-through phone calls and filled a small notebook with reminder notes. Now, she began to write her story—a *backgrounder*—which would help the readers understand what was happening in the county that night. She flipped on the electronic typing terminal on her desk, signaled the typesetting computer to get ready for her story, and began to write:

Like the legendary Peter of Holland, the U.S. Army Corps of Engineers has been trying to save the residents of this county from disaster by plugging a "hole" in the dam with a mile-long "finger" of solid material. Still nervous, however, Corps personnel say they are "aware of distress signs . . . and have been making daily inspections." Now that the rain has exceeded 6 inches [15.24 cm] *in just five hours, they are frankly worried that their cementlike finger cannot hold back the tremendous water pressure building up behind the earthen dam . . .*

By midnight, the reporters at the dam site had called in their stories to the rewrite person and the science editor had finished hers. The city editor edited the backgrounder, using the computer terminal on his desk, and began to work on the stories from the outside reporters as the rewrite person finished them. Barring last-minute big news, the paper would be ready to go to press in another hour, as planned.

Meanwhile, as the Salvation Army and the American Red Cross opened up additional shelters in school gymnasiums, newspersons all over the city were putting their electronic gear and all other tools of their trade to work with the utmost speed, against time and the rising tide of floodwaters, as River City prepared for the worst.

TOOLS AND TECHNIQUES

Reporters, correspondents and stringers all look to their editors for their assignments. Even if their jobs are to cover regular beats, such as the cop shop, their editor is the boss, and may decide to send them somewhere else.

Reporters may, and often do, ask their editors for permission to cover a specific story they find especially interesting. Reporters on regular beats often have *leads*—indications that something is about to happen which is likely to *lead* or develop into a news story—outside their own areas. If the assignment editor likes the idea and thinks it is newsworthy, he or she will ask a general assignment reporter to cover the story. Often a stringer, reporter, or correspondent on a regular beat has a breaking story that is too big for one person to handle, and so, the editor will send a general assignment reporter to help.

General assignment reporting is great for people who like variety. It is an exciting job because one never knows where one will be sent next, or what story one will work on tomorrow. Every day is different, and something new and unexpected always happens. A good general assignment reporter will often have to

do a lot of "homework" when assigned to a story that requires some special background information or knowledge. Of course, if a story necessitates a great deal of specific knowledge or experience, such as a new scientific discovery like the rings around the planet Uranus, a reporter who is already specialized in science would be assigned to cover it. The story would be on his beat.

Working a regular beat—City Hall, business, the governor, or the President of the U.S.—is exciting and satisfying for many news people. A regular assignment to a specific beat makes it possible for the reporter to learn more and more about a specific subject and to explore news stories in those areas in great depth. This is particularly true when working on a newspaper, since there are hundreds of thousands of column inches to fill with news every day. Broadcast news organizations have much less "space" to devote to news, and so, don't need as many specialized reporters, except for all-news radio stations and TV cable all-news networks.

THE TOOLS
OF THE TRADE
All-news radio, TV stations, and networks have actually been made economically practical by the development of lightweight

Television reporters and photographers sometimes use airplanes and helicopters to get to a fast-breaking news scene in a hurry.

45

portable tape recorders. Dubbed *mini-mikes, mini-cams,* and *mini-cassettes,* they are the newest tools in the news reporting trade.

The mini-mike is a cordless microphone which has a miniature FM broadcasting transmitter built into its handle. With the mini-mike, a reporter can plunge into a crowd, roam around a football field, interview people in a large hall, or pick up the voices of newsmakers free of entangling cords. Nearby, usually within half a mile (.80 km) of the reporter, is a mini-FM-receiver connected to a small portable recorder, or a microwave relay which sends the voices picked up by the mini-mike back to the broadcasting station.

The mini-cassette recorder is the basic tool of the radio newsperson. At press conferences, government meetings, or public hearings, sound systems are available, and the radio reporter will often plug the cassette recorder into these systems.

The mini-cam has now almost entirely replaced the film camera as the chosen tool of the television news reporter. With a color TV camera not much larger than an old-fashioned film camera, a video tape recorder strapped on the back or slung over one shoulder and a battery belt fastened around the waist, a TV reporter can often tape on-the-spot news events, all alone. In most cases, though, the TV news is covered by a crew of three: a reporter, a camera person, and someone to supervise the recording of sound. When working with a crew, the reporter is free to concentrate on the primary job of getting the facts of the story, interviewing people, picking up background material, and doing "stand-up reports" in front of the camera. These stand-up reports are often done outside the buildings where important events are happening, to give "atmosphere" to the report.

Both radio and television news reporters and their crews travel in *news cruisers*. These station wagons and small vans are equipped with two-way radios, so the reporters can keep in constant touch with their editors and news directors back at the broadcasting stations.

Television news organizations often use large vans as portable studios. These studios allow them to do high-quality recording of news events on-the-scene. The studios are usually equipped with microwave relays, so that the pictures and sounds of events can be sent back to the TV station via microwave.

Finally, there is always the "good old notebook." No self-respecting reporter, in print or broadcasting, is ever without one. The notebook is the basic and most important tool for newspaper reporters. While many print reporters use cassette recorders to make sure they get their "quotes" right, they depend primarily on their notebooks and some sort of speed-writing or shorthand to get their stories down, until they can get to a typewriter.

The typewriters newspaper reporters use may or may not be the familiar ones that type out words on paper. More and more reporters and editors work on typewriters that type the story into a *computer* which displays what has been written on a *cathode-ray tube* similar to the television screen on your TV sets at home. There is one difference, however. The reporter not only can see what is being written on the CR tube, but can make corrections with a "light pencil" directly on the tube. So the copy on the TV screen can be erased and corrected as easily as if it were written on paper with a pencil. In the same way, the editor can edit copy directly into the computer. In many places, com-

The copydesk at a large newspaper's office. The reporters' stories can be edited electronically on video terminals.

puters have taken over the tedious jobs of setting type, keeping the margins and columns even, and arranging the stories and pictures on the pages of the newspapers.

Back in River City, thousands of people arrived in a steady stream at the armory and the high-school gymnasium. Those who had homes in areas below the dam talked anxiously of the damage floodwaters could bring. The vacationers worried about being stranded in the area and tried to think of ways to let their families know that they were safe. Reporters with their notebooks and electronic gear walked through the crowd, interviewing, taping, and taking pictures. The news that evening was recorded on a great many notebook pages and on countless reels of audio and videotapes. The news of the threat to the River City dam and the story of the evacuation of the people from the low areas was heard and seen across the country. The meaning, and possible prevention, of the impending disaster would be recorded for history.

HOW THE NEWS AFFECTS US

A few years ago, before the days of satellites and worldwide jet air travel, newspersons made up some rules about news belonging to certain categories, that is, local, regional, national, and international. The local news was thought to be of first-rank importance to the "local" audience. The farther away from home a news event occurred, the less important it was thought to be to the home audience.

We are now aware, however, that a meeting of bankers in Zurich, Switzerland, can affect the supermarket on the corner, by raising the price of hot dogs still another dime. Unseasonable weather in Brazil can cause an increase in the price of a cup of coffee or hot chocolate in St. Louis, Missouri. Everything in our world today seems to be connected to everything else. Droughts, war, or threats of war, changes of governments, and riots in one part of the world will be sorely felt in every other part as well. This is why we see so much "international" news in our local newspaper and on our local TV station. The best journalists feel that it is their job to make the connections for us between what is happening in our world and what the happening may mean for each of us, personally.

One of our great journalists, former CBS News chief Fred W. Friendly, has said, "What makes the modern-day journalist essential is his or her ability to explain . . . to provide a picture of reality on which members of society can act."

DEMOCRACY, THE NEWS, AND YOU

You are growing up in a society that will expect you, at age eighteen, to know enough about what is going on in your community, your state, and your nation to enter into the democratic process of governing yourself. When that day comes, you will have to act on a picture of reality that is provided for you by the news. It is never too early to start paying attention to the news and to begin to ask your reporters and editors, "What does it mean?"

It is not always obvious what the news really does mean. But, it is the mission of our journalists to find out. It is their job to go to whatever specialists they can find and to pull together as much information as possible. Watergate, the Energy Crisis, Three Mile Island—we have to know what they *mean* in order to survive as a free people.

HOW OUR NEWS CAN AFFECT THE WORLD

In the very early hours of the morning on Sunday, November 6, 1977, the small community of Toccoa, Georgia, was shocked to learn that the nearby Kelly Barnes Dam had collapsed and sent a wall of water equal in weight to 7,500 freight train locomotives rushing downstream to wreck a college campus and take 39 human lives—20 of them children.

The news from this small community reached the President of the United States that same day, and just a few days later, he ordered a federal program of dam inspection to begin immediately. Responding to that presidential order, the U.S. Army Corps of Engineers found and repaired dozens of leaky dams including Addicks and Barker dams just above Houston, Texas, with its population of well over a million people. At one time, just before these dams were repaired, Houston had 10 inches (25.40 cm) of rain in a twenty-four hour period, and was threatened with a dam disaster like the one used in this book to illustrate how news stories develop. In fact, as news of the disaster near the little town of Toccoa spread to the rest of the world, citizens of many areas that were downstream from dams realized that they must see to it that their own nearby dams must be checked and made safe before their communities faced a similar disaster.

It stopped raining, finally, at a few minutes past one o'clock, Saturday afternoon.

By the time the city editor of the local newspaper got to his desk at three o'clock and settled into the routine of getting together the news for the Sunday edition, the weather bureau was reporting that slightly more than 10 inches (25.40 cm) of rain had fallen.

Across the city, the assignment editor at the television station checked the stories scheduled for the six o'clock news, which included the good news that the repair work begun by the U.S. Army Corps of Engineers had probably saved the city from a major disaster.

An anchorperson at a city radio station finished her five

minutes of hourly news at 3:05 P.M. with the good news and reached for her telephone to call her wire service to give them the latest update.

It was Sunday morning in Australia at the time, on the other side of the globe. A radio newscaster in Hobart, the capital city of the state of Tasmania, Australia, was preparing his early morning news. He spotted a brief wire story on his teletype machine about the dam scare in River City, U.S.A.

"Great," he mumbled as he tore the wire copy off the machine. "This is just the thing to get our people checking on those old dams on the central plateau." He added the story to the others for his next newscast.

By the time church services were over on Sunday, the dam story was about wrapped up. And it was at the very moment that the anchorwoman in River City stapled together all the copy of the dam story to be filed in the morgue file that she received the call.

"Chris Wood, here. Get yourself ready. A big one just broke. Someone stole the Marland diamond from the museum not five minutes ago."

The anchorwoman dropped the copy into the file and cued up the recorder.

"OK, Chris, go ahead. The tape's rolling."

Reporting "from the scene" on the first moon landing, astronaut Edwin Aldrin turned reporter to bring us news about the moon.

FOR FURTHER READING

Bendick, Jeanne. *TV Reporting* (Finding Out About Jobs). New York: Parents' Magazine Press, 1976.

Friendly, F. W. *Due to Circumstances Beyond Our Control.* New York: Random House, 1967.

Jackson, G. *Getting into Broadcast Journalism.* New York: Hawthorne, 1974.

Meyer, G. P. *Pioneers of the Press.* Chicago: Rand McNally, 1961.

Miles, D. W. *Broadcast News Handbook.* Indianapolis: Howard S. Sams, 1975.

Myers, Hortense, and Murrow, Edward R. *Young Newscaster.* Indianapolis: Bobbs-Merrill, 1951.

Pope, Billy M. *Let's Visit a Newspaper.* New York: Taylor Publishing, 1971.

Siller, R. C. *Radio and TV News Guide to Professional Radio and TV Newscasting.* Blue Ridge Summit, Pa., Tab Books, Inc. 1972.

Taylor, Paula. *Walter Cronkite, This Is Walter Cronkite.* Chicago: Children's Press, 1975.

Wolverton, Mike. *And Now the News.* Houston: Gulf Publishing, 1977.

INDEX

Acta Diurna, 5
Actualities, 23–24
Advisories, 40
Affiliates, 17, 18
Aldrin, Edwin, 54
"All Things Considered," 25
Anchorpersons, 1–2, 25. *See also* Radio; Television
Associated Press (AP), 17

Beats, 14, 45
Bombeck, Erma, 28
Boston, first newspaper in, 6
Bracken, Peg, 29
Broadcasting, 23–26ff., 46–47. *See also* Radio; Television
"Broadcast journalists," 11
Bureaus, news, 17

Carter, Jimmy, 25
Cathode ray tube, 47
China, ancient, 5
City editor, 38ff.
Columns and columnists, 28
Composing room, 31
Computers, 47–48
"Cop shop," 14
Copydesk, 48
Crawl, 38
Cronkite, Walter, 30

Dams, 2, 8–9, 21, 33–42, 48, 52–55
Democracy, 52
Documentaries, 24, 25
Drums, to relay news, 5

Editorials, 29
Editors, 12ff., 38ff.
Electronic equipment, 30–31
    See also Computers
Equal time, 30

Fairness Doctrine, 30
Floods. See Dams
Franklin, Benjamin, 6
Friendly, Fred W., 52

General assignment, 16, 43–44
Gutenberg, Johannes, 5–6

Helicopters, 44
Heloise, 29
History, 4–9
Hot line, 40

Information, as news, 3–4
International news, 51–52

Journalists, 11–12ff., 51–52

Landers, Ann, 29
Lead-in, 34
Leads, 43

Letters to the editor, 28

Magazines, news, 6, 7
    television, 26
Messengers, 5
Microwave, 26, 37, 46
Mini-cams, 46
Mini-cassettes, 46
Mini-mikes, 46
Military expeditions, and news, 5
Montgomery, Ala., bus boycott, 8
Moon landing, 54
Morgue, 2

Networks, 17, 18
Newsbreaks, 24
News bureaus, 17
Newscasters. See Anchorpersons
News cruisers, 47
News flashes, 7
News magazines. See Magazines
Newspapers, 5–6, 7, 16, 26–27ff., 45, 47–48. See also specific jobs
News services, 17–18
Notebooks, 47

Olden times, news in, 4–5

Parks, Rosa, 8
Peking Gazette, 5
Pennsylvania Gazette, 6
Pictographs, 5
Police beat, 14
Pressroom, 28
Print media. *See* Newspapers
"Print journalists," 11
Publick Occurrences, 6

Radio, 6, 7, 23–24, 25. *See also* Broadcasting; specific jobs
Reporters, 14, 15, 43ff. *See also* specific media
Reuters International, 17
Rewrite person, 14

Satellites, 6
Ship crews, and news, 5
Side bars, 15
Signals, 5
Sixty Minutes, 26
Slant, editorial, 29
Smoke signals, 5
Snowfall, 3
Special correspondents, 16

Stamberg, Susan, 25
Stringers, 12–13

Tape recorders (videotape), 13, 18, 46
Telegraph, 6
Telephone, 6
    hot line, 40
Teletype machines, 17–18
Television, 6, 7, 13, 15, 16, 18, 20, 24–25, 37, 44. *See also* Broadcasting; specific jobs
Toccoa, Ga., 52–53
Tsing-Pao, 5
Typewriters, 47

United Press International (UPI), 17
Unusual happenings, 2–3

Vanderbilt, Amy, 29
Videotape. *See* Tape recorders
Villages, and news, 4–5
Voice over, 15
Voicer, 34

Warnings, as news, 4
Wire services, 17–19